THE FIVE HUSBANDS THAT DON'T BELONG TO YOU!

I0108105

BY MADELINE KNIGHT

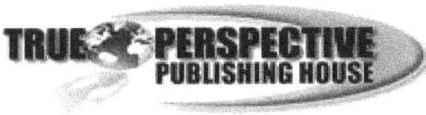

TRUE PERSPECTIVE PUBLISHING HOUSE

~ <u>The Five Husbands That Don't Belong To You!</u> ~

~ II ~

Special thanks to Samuel Ramirez for cover design and bio picture. Thank you for being sensitive and led by the Holy Spirit to put together the vision the Lord put in my heart.

WE ARE THE KINGDOM
ENTERTAINMENT

AUTOGRAPH PAGE

Autograph this book as a personal investment to a
woman that God has put in your path on this life journey.

~ <u>The Five Husbands That Don't Belong To You!</u> ~

~ VI ~

Acknowledgments

I thank my Lord and Savior Jesus for bringing this freedom, healing and restoration to my life, the life He has given me. Where would I be without Him? May I always bring glory to Your name as I don't take lightly what you have allowed me to do in this hour and season. It's an honor and a privilege to be the vessel You use to manifest Your presence.

I thank and bless God for my parents Miguel Colon and Milagros Pena for presenting me to the Lord at a young age, praying me through and for the encouragement and love.

I thank and bless my daughters Nia and Adalia, the two Jesus girls that God has given me. Thank you Nia and Adalia for being mommies cheerleaders.

I thank and bless my local church, *Light to the Nations International Ministry*, led by Apostle Ruth Serrano and Pastor Wilmer Rodriguez. Apostle Ruth, thank you for pushing me, stretching me and believing in me. Thank you for showing me in your own life what true devotion to the Lord really is and for helping me grow and develop in different areas of ministry. I thank you for your prayers in my favor and my families favor. I thank God the Lord used you to reveal a missing piece I needed to add to this book.

I thank my Grandfather in the Faith Sam Cotto for declaring the prophetic word over my life; that this was the season and time to write this book. I bless your beautiful wife and children. Thank you man of God!

There were a lot of people that God used along the way to get me to this point. Many prophetic words were spoken and much wise council and many declarations were received. But a special thank you to Prophet Maria Fernanda for being sensitive to the Lord and helping me get out of the pit these Husbands had me in. Thank you woman of God for declaring to me who I was in the Lord. Thank you for believing in me when I didn't even believe in myself.

Blessing to my Brother Miguel and my sister in law Jackie and my nephews Julian and Tayey. Blessing and thanks to all the leaders and Brothers and Sisters of *Light to the Nations International Ministry* for all their prayers and support. Thank you Sammy for helping me create what is today the Kingdom Key collection. I would have never been able to do it without you.   May God bless you and your family continually.

Thank you Jackie and Rodney Brown for your continual support and love. May God bless you Ozzie Mae Culmer and Greg Culmer, for the encouraging and wise council you brought me and Rod. Please don't get offended if I left anyone out but may the Lord reward your labor of love!

~<u>The Five Husbands That Don't Belong To You!</u> ~

~ X ~

SPECIAL THANKS

A special thank you to my spiritual parents Apostle Ruth Serrano Rodriguez and Pastor Wilmer Rodriguez. Thank you for imparting into my life paternity, prayer, love, the word of God and wise council. May God bless your labor of love!

Ministerio Internacional
Luz a las Naciones

Special thanks to Vanessa Rodriguez at avrmipaz@ yahoo.com for hair and make-up. God Bless you Woman of God.

Special thanks to the Man of God the Lord has blessed me with, my Husband Rodrick Knight. I bless God for your patience, your attentiveness, your wise council and above all else, love. I thank you for understanding the call of God over my life and releasing me to do the will of the Father. I know that the short term tribulation created a weight of glory, not only over me, but also over our marriage and family.

l love you!

MY MISSION AND VISION

Mission- My mission as a Representative of the Kingdom of God and with the keys he has given me is to unlock woman from any jail cell they may be in weather the name of the jail cell be called Rejection, Anger, Bitterness, Unforgiveness, Loneliness or Death so they can regain their value again.

Vision- My Vision is too see Woman free, healed, and restored back to GOD. So they can also become like the Samaritan woman walking in the destiny and plans God established by announcing to the world come see this man that has told me everything I ever did!

~<u>The Five Husbands That Don't Belong To You!</u> ~

TABLE OF CONTENTS

INTRODUCTION

I was like the woman in the front of this book cover, looking at my reflection in that water that day at the well and not being happy with what I saw. I saw Rejection, Anger, Bitterness, Unforgiveness, Loneliness, Death and not only were they in me but surrounding me.

It was how the Holy Spirit of God revealed to me my condition during my two year separation from My Husband. I was trying to move on with life, but I had been intimate and associated myself physically, emotionally and spiritually to these Five Husbands that did not belong to me and they were still surrounding me. When I looked up the word *Intimacy- it means close or warm friendship or understanding;* personal relationship, and this personal relationship that was developed with these five husbands left me feeling bound, sick, unloved, unhappy, and incomplete. I needed Freedom, I needed Healing, I needed Restoration, and I needed to feel Complete.

ᰮᰮᰮᰮ

How did I get here? What had affected me to such magnitude?

BETRAYAL!

Definition of Betrayal-To deliver into hands of an enemy in violation of trust or allegiance. To be false or disloyal, to deceive

<u>When Betrayal comes through your back door!</u>

Betrayal had opened the back door of my home and came in and destroyed my marriage. I remember having a dream prior to discovering my husband infidelity that a big Giant in a form of man was coming in through the back sliding doors of my home. His appearance was horrific like he was ready to kill, steal, and destroy. In the dream I saw myself grabbing my two daughters and a phone in other hand and I heard myself telling that Giant you better not come in. But now I understand that in that dream I never protected my husband or my marriage.

~ XVIII ~

Luke 12:39 Know this: A homeowner who knew exactly when a burglar was coming would not permit the house to be broken into.

I was being alerted by the Holy Spirit that my house (My Marriage) was going to be broken into. I also dreamed that I was speaking to my husband in our kitchen and seeing bullet holes all over him. Betrayal did come and destroyed my marriage and my family and destroyed me as a woman. What you are about to read is my personal encounter with these husbands during my two year separation. You will read how Jesus revealed to me what each one of them individually had done to me. Most importantly how I could be made free from each and every one of them and kill them from my life so they can never recover again.

Throughout the book I will be using the word *Reveal or Revelation which means the making known of a secret or the unknown.* Jesus arrived at the well to *reveal* to me the truth about these husbands and the harm they were causing me and what I needed to be free from them. I've learned when you receive *revelation,* your life does not stay the same. Revelation brings freedom! So there is freedom in what you are about to read in this book because it has enough revelation to change your life.

Before you read the revelation that Jesus gave me for these husband's that I was being intimate with, you will see throughout this book that I will making declarations to you. I want to explain to you what that means.

The definition of Declaration- the formal announcement of the beginning of a state or condition.

So I declare that this is the beginning to your new state and condition because your Freedom is about to begin. I am going to declare it again, your Freedom is about to begin; your about to meet the same Jesus I met by my well, that Jesus that talked to me and told me everything I should know!

~ XX ~

THE BLANK CHECK ARRIVES!

THE BLANK CHECK HAS ARRRIVED! When the Holy Spirit of God led me to this bible story, I've read it many times but this time the Holy Spirit revealed to me that the Samaritan woman in this story was me! Let me introduce you to the conversation that not only changed the course of this Samaritan woman life but it changed the course of my Life. Why do I say blank check (thank you Sean) because Jesus was on his way to bring her back her value, the value that these Five Husbands had stolen from her was about to be recovered.

What is Value-The regard that something is held to deserve, the importance, worth, or usefulness of something.

Declaration!

I declare in the name of Jesus that your value is about to be recovered. Yes, you reading this book, you are not reading this book by coincidence but Jesus has arrived where ever you may be right now to remind you how important and valuable you are!

~ XXI ~

~The Five Husbands That Don't Belong To You! ~

JOHN 4:174 He had to go through Samaria on the way.5 Eventually he came to the Samaritan village of Sychar, near the parcel of ground that Jacob gave to his son Joseph.6 Jacob's well was there; and Jesus, tired from the long walk, sat wearily beside the well about noontime.7 Soon a Samaritan woman came to draw water, and Jesus said to her, Please give me a drink.8 He was alone at the time because his disciples had gone into the village to buy some food.9 The woman surprised, for Jews refuse to have anything to do with Samaritans. She said to Jesus, You are a Jew, and I am a Samaritan woman. Why are you asking me for a drink?10 Jesus replied, If you only knew the gift God has for you and who I am, you would ask me, and I would give you living water.11 But sir , you don't have a rope or a bucket, she said, and this is a very deep well. Where would you get this living water? 12 And besides, are you greater than our ancestor Jacob who gave us this well? How can you offer better water than he and his sons and his cattle enjoyed?13 Jesus replied, people soon become thirsty again after drinking this water.14 But the water I give them takes away thirst altogether. It becomes a perpetual spring within them, going them eternal life."15 Please sir, the woman said, give me some of that water!

Then I'll never be thirsty again, and I won't have to come here to haul water.16 Go and get your husband, Jesus told her.17 I don't have a husband, the woman replied. Jesus said, You're right! You don't have a husband- 18 for you have had five husbands, and you aren't even married to the man you're living with now.

URGENT, AND HE HAD TO GO THROUGH SAMARIA!

Oh how I love Jesus's urgency to get to this woman. Verse 4 says He had to go through Samaria. That's how important this woman was to him. There was an urgency to SEEK and SAVE her; these are the two words came to my heart when I read this story. I looked up both words in the dictionary and *Seek* means *to obtain or reach* and *save* means *to keep safe or rescue*. I, like this Samaritan woman needed Jesus to pass by the city of Gibsonton to *reach* me and *save* me.

Luke 19:10 For the Son of Man came to seek and save that which was lost.

HE UNDERSTANDS!

It caught my attention that even before the Samaritan woman arrived at the well it says in verse 6, Jesus tired from the long walk, sat wearily beside the well about noontime. Jesus was already feeling the condition of this woman, her tiredness and weariness. How long of a journey it had been for her and how these husbands had left her.

Hebrews 4:15 says, *"This High Priest of ours understands our weaknesses, for he faced all of the same testing's we do, yet he did not sin. It reminds me how badly I wanted someone to understand how weak I was feeling, how incomplete this betrayal had left me, and I how I no longer felt valuable."*

BUT NOONTIME ARRIVED!

I love how everything in the bible has so much meaning even time Jesus sat by that well, it says it was noontime. The biblical meaning of the number 12 is completeness which means having everything that is needed and to make whole. There was a wholeness coming to my life and to this Samaritan women that we were not expecting to receive.

Declaration!

I declare in the name Of Jesus to each person reading this book that your noon time has arrived. The same Man that came to rescue me and save me, is also here for you to rescue you and save you. He has arrived to bring you completeness that means everything you need will be provided. I declare it's your noon time, I am going to say it again it's your noon time, time to talk to Jesus and receive wholeness that he can only bring to you! Let it begin!

~ XXV ~

Chapter 1

The Husband named Rejection

When I looked up the word *rejection* it says, *to discard as defective or useless, throw away!* And I definitely felt discarded, defective, and useless and that I had been thrown away.

BEING REFUSED!

John 4:9 The woman was surprised, for Jews refuse to have anything to do with Samaritans, She said to

Jesus, You are a Jew, and I am a Samaritan woman. Why are you asking me for a drink?

See it says that the Jews refused to have anything to do with Samaritans. The Samaritan woman was saying Jesus why are you talking to me don't you understand that I have been refused (rejected), I am defective, there is something wrong with me. I don't have anything to offer to you or anybody.

What I experienced is when you are refused it leaves you feeling useless. When you have intimacy with this **Husband of Rejection** this husband leaves you feeling that something is wrong with you. I us to say it all the time, what is wrong me, what's wrong with me. *Rejection* had left me with a low self-esteem, I like this Samaritan woman became full of insecurities, the way I looked became a problem since I felt that I was not enough woman for my Husband because if I would have been enough he would not have been unfaithful to me. That was the way rejection left me feeling and thinking. I remember cutting my hair, changing my hair color, buying new clothes because I wanted to feel better, but my condition was just getting worse. It had gotten so bad that I went to see a Doctor.

I told the Doctor I don't feel like myself, I feel anxious, overwhelmed; even attending to my two daughters felt overwhelming. I could not sleep and I was always crying. What I was experiencing was the symptoms that *rejection* left me. The doctor had diagnosed me, gave me an anti-depression pill and sent me on my way. But instead of the anti-depression pill making me better, that pill made me feel worse and my condition worsened.

HE CHOSE US!

I can imagine that Samaritan woman saying to Jesus, a gift for me! Jesus you don't understand I have just been used up. How can God have a gift for me? I am not precious enough to receive a gift. Jesus was telling her I know how you feel as I was also *rejected.* But I was precious to God because He chooses me.

1 Peter 2:4 Come to Christ, who is the living cornerstone of God's temple. He was REJECTED by people, But he is PRECIOUS TO GOD WHO CHOSE HIM. Thanks be to God who chooses us!

THE WATER HAS ARRIVED!

John 4:10 If you only knew the gift God has for you and who I am, you would ask me, and I would give you living water.

Jesus was telling the Samaritan woman, see I am here to bring you something. This gift that I am here to give you, this world that no human being can give you. I came to bring you life! Why do I say life because He offered her living water. Jesus was saying to me and this Samaritan woman you are dehydrated. *Dehydrated* means to *remove water from.* Jesus said to me that's what happened to you Madeline and this Samaritan woman. The **Husband of Rejection** had removed life from you! But Jesus said I have come to bring you life again.

John 10:10 The thief comes only to steal and kill and destroy. I came that they may have LIFE and have it ABUNDANTLY.

Jesus said the **Husband of Rejection** has stolen from you and killed you and destroyed you long enough. I have come to give you life and not only life but life abundantly. Jesus said I've come to remind you who you are in Me; that you are my Masterpiece. The word Masterpiece means an artist's or craftsman's best piece of work. I could imagine this Samaritan woman saying to Jesus, me because I was also thinking the same thing. How do you see me as your best piece of work? Have you looked at me Jesus, I am a mess! But Jesus said, no you are not a mess you are My Masterpiece Madeline. How I needed to hear that from Jesus. I needed to hear that I was beautiful, that I was special and that I was His best work.

Ephesians 2:10 for we are God's masterpiece. He has created us a new in Christ Jesus, so we can do the good things He planned for us long ago.

THE BLACK AND WHITE HEEL!

While I was experiencing *rejection,* I was invited by my Apostle, Ruth Serrano to a service in Orlando Florida. On my way to the service, I was saying in my heart I would love a pair of black and white heels. When the Apostle and I arrived at the service we sat together. While service was going on, I saw her slipping of her heels and my Apostle said to me that these are for you. Yes they were black and white heels and they were brand new! I bless her life because it wasn't the shoes that were important but it was Jesus telling me I am here, I have not left you and I have not abandoned you. You are still my Masterpiece and no *rejection* could take that away! I remember driving back alone in my car just crying! And the Lords sweet whisper to my heart was saying your husband may have *rejected* you and people might not see your value but I haven't *rejected* you Madeline. I am still here and you are valuable to me.

Declaration!

I am here to let you know that you have been chosen by God and I declare this abundant life that only Jesus can offer you. Now over your life I call incompleteness out and call an abundance of completeness over you. I am here to remind you that you are God's masterpiece, fearfully and wonderfully made by Him and for Him!

Repeat with me!

In the name of Jesus I will no longer be intimate with *rejection* because I am accepting the abundant life Jesus has come to give me; that means I have value and I am His masterpiece.

Chapter 2

HUSBAND NAMED ANGER!

Definition of *Anger, a strong feeling of displeasure aroused by wrong!* John 4: 11-12 But sir, you don't have a rope or a bucket, she said, and this is a very deep well. Where would you get this living water? And besides, are you greater than our ancestors Jacob who gave us this well? How can you offer better water than he and his sons and his cattle enjoyed.

Look at this woman's response to Jesus. She was saying how can You possibly offer me something better than the **Husband of Anger** that I have been intimate with.,

LETTING THE SUN GO DOWN ON MY ANGER!

Ephesians 4:26-27 and don't sin by letting Anger gain control over you. Don't let the sun go down while you are still angry, for anger gives a mighty foothold to the Devil.

I remember being so *angry* at my husband that my daily life was full of irritation, frustration and rage. This **Husband of Anger** continually told me to get revenge, go get even; it had gained control of me and caused the Devil to have a mighty foot hold in my life. I looked up the word *foothold* and it means *a firm secure position that provides a base for further advancement.* And *anger* had definitely given advancement to the devil in my life.

WHEN ANGER LEADS YOU TO SIN!

This is the way the Holy Spirit of God revealed it to me while writing this book. The Holy spirit of God revealed to me that *anger* leads you to make wrong decisions. *Anger* told me get a divorce and you will find someone else, go back to the world, go back to the night clubs, join the dating scene, go back to alcohol, show your husband you don't need him anymore. I say go back, go back because I had been there once before!

James 2-19 My dear brothers and sisters be quick to listen, slow to speak, and slow to get angry.

Your *anger* can never make things right in God's sight. I and this Samaritan woman were not being quick to listen to Jesus or being slow to get *angry*. I, like this Samaritan woman thought *anger* would make things right but it didn't. *Anger* led me to go back, back to sin. I was like this Samaritan woman speaking about a deep well because my life was in a deep pit of sin, the alcohol, the dating and the divorce papers that I started. None of those things were working and I was in a pit of sin and I needed Jesus to get me out.

Psalm 103:4 (AMP) Who redeems your life from the pit and corruption, who beautifies, dignifies, and crowns you with loving-kindness and tender mercy.

Anger had me so focus on revenge, get even that I had forgotten about and love.

Corinthians 1:3-5 (AMP) Love (God's love in us)does no insist on its own rights or its own way, for it is not self-seeking; it is not touchy or fretful or resentful; it takes no account of the evil done to it(it pays no attention to a suffered wrong.

How I needed God's love; how this Samaritan woman also needed God's love. I remember driving in my car and God's Holy Spirit tugging at my heart saying Madeline, you giving and showing love depends on how you have been treated or are being treated or how you feel. But my Love in you does not depend on how someone treats you or what they have done to you or how you feel. When you have my love in you, you don't focus on the wrong done by another because my love covers any wrong.

1 PETER 4:8 Most important of all, continue to show deep love for each other, for love covers a multitude of sin.

Jesus was saying to me, like He was telling the Samaritan woman, I am here to give you my love that will cover any *anger* in your life and when you receive my love you are able to cover any wrong. This is what it means to be a blessing to those who have been unkind.

1 PETER 4:9 Don't repay evil for evil. Don't retaliate when people say unkind things about you. Instead, pay them back with a blessing. That is what God wants you to do, and he will bless you for it.

Jesus was telling me and this Samaritan woman now instead of repaying those people that rejected you or hurt you with *anger,* you will now repay all evil you have experienced with My love.

DECLARATION!

While you are reading this book I declare that you will start to feel God's love. It has arrived to heal that anger in your life. I don't know what caused this anger, it might not be a betrayal like it was for me. But He is ready to give you His love that covers a multitude of sins, receive it!

~ 13 ~

Repeat with me!

In Jesus name I will no longer live in *anger* and I will no longer let this *anger* rule my life and my decision making. I receive this love that only Jesus can give me to cover the multitude of wrongs.

Chapter 3

THE HUSBAND CALLED BITTERNESS

Refuse to drink the water of bitterness! See when you have had intimacy with the *Husband of Anger* he introduces you to the *Husband of Bitterness*. The definition of *bitter* is *resentment; a feeling of deep anger and ill-will.*

~ 15 ~

Jesus was telling me and this Samaritan woman, look what happens when you do not refuse to drink *bitterness.*

Mathew 27:34 The soldiers gave him wine mixed with bitter gall, but when he had tasted it, He refused to drink it!

I DRANK BITTERNESS!

I realized that I did not refuse to drink *bitterness* and I drank from that sponge and it influenced me to make decisions like move out from the home that me and my husband had together with our two daughters. I took my two daughters and isolated myself to a small apartment. This *bitterness* had taken root in me and corrupted me and made me not believe anymore in anything or anyone.

Hebrew 12:15 Look after each other so that none of you will miss out on the special favor of God. Watch out that no bitter root of unbelief rises up among you, for whenever it springs up; many are corrupted by its poison.

Poison is a substance that, when introduced into or absorbed by a living organism, causes death or injury. This poison that I absorbed got into my system so much that not only was I feeling like I was dying but I was causing so much injury to my daughters as well.   I was not functioning as mother to them. I was so bitter that I resented my husband for leaving me to be a single mother. I was bitter that I was left to do it on my own. I felt that life was cheating me.

But Jesus said to me like He said to this woman:

John 4:13-14 People soon become thirsty again after drinking this water. But the water I give takes away thirst altogether. It becomes a perpetual spring within them, giving them eternal life.

INTRODUCED TO THE CARPENTER!

Jesus was saying you have drunk from the sponge of *bitterness* and it has left you thirsty, it's not quenching your thirst, it's not bringing any satisfaction to your life. That is the place where you are at right now and it is called Marah! I am sure this woman was saying Marah, Jesus what do you mean?

Exodus 15-23 When they came to Marah, they finally found water. But the people couldn't drink it because it was bitter. (That is why the place was called Marah, which means bitter.) 25 So Moses cried out to the Lord for help, and the Lord showed him a branch. Moses took the branch and threw it into the water. This made the water good to drink.

Jesus was saying to the Samaritan woman as He said to me, let me reveal to you who I am.

Mark 6:2-3 The next Sabbath he began teaching in the synagogue, and many who heard him were astonished. They asked, "Where did he get all this wisdom and the power to perform miracles? He's just the CARPENTER!

I soon realized that my heart was so full of *bitterness* and that I could not share in the joy of being a mother to my daughters or enjoy anything around me because of my condition. And the solution to this bitterness was in the

Carpenter Jesus and I needed this Carpenter to throw a piece of wood in my water to make me good again.

DECLARATION!

I declare the Carpenter named Jesus has arrived to change your Marah *(bitterness)* to good water. I declare this good water will quench your thirst and it becomes a perpetual spring giving you eternal life. I shout the Words that Jesus said in *John 7:37-38 If you are thirsty, come and drink! If you believe in him come and drink! He is the piece of wood to make your water good again.*

REPEAT WITH ME!

I will not drink from the sponge of *bitterness* any longer. I will not drink that poison anymore but I ask you Jesus as my Carpenter to throw the wood I need to make me good again!

Chapter 4

THE HUSBAND NAMED UNFORGIVENESS

Definition of u*nforgiveness; a grudge against someone who has offended you.*

John 4:15 Please, sir the woman said, give me some of that water! Then I'll never be thirsty again, and I won't have to come here to haul water."

I needed this water of forgiveness and this Samaritan woman needed the water of forgiveness. Because *The Husband of Bitterness* had introduced me to the *Husband*

~ 21 ~

named Unforgiveness, what I experienced is that once you drink from bitterness it's hard to forgive. Since I drank from the sponge bitterness I was unable to say what Jesus said on the cross when they were crucifying Him. I was unable to say Father forgive them for they don't know what they are doing! What I learned is that when people reject us; make us angry and bitter we feel like they owe us something. Oh and how I felt that my husband owed me something!

Jesus was telling me like He was telling the Samaritan woman look at yourself you have let this ***Husband of Unforgiveness*** put you in a prison! And that is exactly how I felt in my daily life, like I was a prisoner in a jail cell. Jesus sat down at my well just like He sat down with this Samaritan woman and said let me reveal to you what *unforgiveness* does and what forgiveness can bring you!

Mathew 18: 23-27 Therefore, the kingdom of Heaven can be compared to a king who decided to bring his accounts up to date with servants who had borrowed money from him. In the process, one of his debtors was brought in who owed him millions of dollars. He couldn't pay, so his master ordered that he be sold- along with his wife, his children, and everything he owned- to pay the debt. But the man fell down before his master and begged him, please, be patient with me, and I will pay it all. Then the master was filled with pity for him, and he released him and forgave his debt.

This King was honoring the servants request to forgive a huge debt he owed. But now let's see this same servant reaction to someone that asked him to forgive his debt.

Mathew 18:28 But when the man left the king, he went to a fellow servant who owed him a few thousand dollars. He grabbed him by the throat and demanded instant payment.

Look at this servant's reaction. He was just forgiven but he was unwilling to forgive. Jesus said to me that's how you were Madeline demanding that your husband pay for his betrayal unwilling to forgive his debt, when I forgave your debt.

Mathew 18:29-30 His fellow servant fell down before him and begged for a little more time. Be patient with me, and I will pay it, he pleaded. But his creditor (and I was the creditor) wouldn't wait. He had the man arrested and put in prison until the debt could be paid in full.

I realized in my heart that I had thrown my husband in prison by not forgiving his debt.

Mathew 18: 31 When some of the other servants saw this, they were very upset. They went to the king and told him everything that had happened. Then he king called in the man he had forgiven and said 'You evil servant! I forgave you that tremendous debt because you pleaded with me. Shouldn't you have mercy on your fellow servant, just as I had mercy on you?

It was true, this Samaritan woman and I had been forgiven by Jesus He had come to our well offering us the water of forgiveness, and we didn't do anything to deserve that Gift. Here we were pleading for this water so that we would never be thirsty again and all we had to do was forgive. Jesus said to me this is the results of *unforgiveness.*

Mathew 18:34 Then the angry king sent the man to prison to be tortured until he had paid his entire debt.

Jesus said, "Madeline this is what happens when you don't _forgive._ . Not only the person that you have not forgiven ends up in a prison but also you end up in a prison yourself, your heart, your mind and your soul. So you have to forgive your husband in your heart."

Mathew 18:35 That's what my heavenly Father will do to you if you refuse to forgive your brothers and sisters from your heart.

FORGIVE, FORGIVE, AND FORGIVE!

I remember leaving a church service and feeling a strong push that this was the night I needed to tell my husband that I forgave him. I kept telling the Lord in the car, Lord but he betrayed me, he hurt me, he was unfaithful to me. Why can't he tell me please forgive me Madeline for betraying you, for hurting you, for causing you all this pain? But inside of me I knew and I know the Lord knew that even if he said those words to me I would not had released him from the prison I had put him in. The Lord said, "Tonight Madeline release him and yourself out of the prison". I rang the doorbell where he was, as soon as he opened the door I started to cry and scream, "I forgive you, I forgive you!" And I learned that it was not going to be my last time saying this. I've learned from that night that forgiveness has to be continually in our mouth so when *unforgiveness* arrives to have intimacy with you; you are able to say no I have already had intimacy with forgiveness.

Ephesians 4:31 Get rid of all bitterness, rage, anger, harsh words, and slander, as well as all types of malicious behavior. Instead, be kind to each other, tenderhearted, forgiving one another, just as God through Christ has forgiven you.

DECLARATION!

I declare that you are able to drink from the water that Jesus is offering you today, the water of forgiveness and with this water you are able to forgive anyone who has offended you. Remember the Lord has forgiven you! So I challenge you to release yourself and your debtors out of prison, and forgive!

REPEAT WITH ME!

Lord Jesus today I forgive all those who rejected me, hurt me, and mistreated me with their actions or words and I release them and myself from any prison of *unforgiveness;* today I forgive because I have been forgiven, in Jesus name AMEN!

Chapter 5

HUSBAND NAMED LONELINESS!

Definition of *loneliness; the state of being alone in solitary isolation.*

I could relate to this Samaritan woman as result of being intimate with this **Husband of Loneliness** as I had put up a lot of walls to protect myself from people. I didn't want to get close to anybody because I did not want to get hurt again. And the Lord revealed it to me this way, He said, "Madeline you are in a remote and barren place but I am going to show you the ingredient you need to get out!"

Mathew 14: 15-20 AMP When evening came, the disciples came to him and said, This is a remote and barren place, and the day is now over; send the throngs (people) away into the villages to buy food for themselves. Jesus said they do not need to go away; you give them something to eat. They said to him, we have nothing here but five loaves and two fish. He said, bring them here to me. Then he ordered the crowds to recline on the grass; and He took the five loaves and the two fish, and, looking up to heaven, He gave thanks and blessed and broke the loaves and handed the pieces to the disciples, and the disciples gave them to the people. And they all ate and were satisfied.

I love the word satisfied. I had not felt satisfied in a long time. I looked up the word r*emote* and it means *hiding away* and that is just what I did, I hid myself from everything and everyone. I also looked up b*arren* and it means *being incapable of producing.* The bareness had left me incapable of producing anything.

JESUS WITH THE BREAD OF LIFE AND GRACE!

Jesus said to me and this Samaritan Woman I am here to offer you bread so you can live! I love that throughout this whole conversation that Jesus had with the Samaritan woman He kept offering her Life!

John 6:51 I am the living bread that came down out of heaven. Anyone who eats this bread will live forever; this bread is my flesh, offered so the world may live.

I needed this bread as the next husband. He did not just want to be intimate with me but wanted to take my life. Jesus was not only at this well to offer me and the Samaritan woman this Bread but He was there to share with me the meaning of the Five Breads. The announcement came from Jesus saying, woman I came to bring you favor which means *undeserved acceptance and love received from another*. Jesus said to me, "You know why Madeline the disciples felt that they did not have enough to feed the people? Because no human being or thing can bring you true satisfaction, or acceptance, or love, not even your husband, nor your children, not even your job or money. But when you eat

~ 31 ~

the Bread that I can only offer you, you feel fertile again, productive and you feel satisfied.

DECLARATION

I declare that time of isolation is over for you. That you will no longer remain in a state that is *barren* or in a *remote* place, because Jesus has arrived to give His Bread and His Favor, so you no longer have to be intimate with the **Husband of Loneliness.** I announce to you life, acceptance and love has arrived. If you eat from this Bread, it will produce in your life true satisfaction, the only satisfaction that Jesus can bring to you, so your life can feel and be productive again.

REPEAT WITH ME!

Lord Jesus I receive this bread that is Your flesh because I want to live, I want to be accepted and I want Your love. I want that true satisfaction that comes from You. So I will eat Your bread as a sign that I will not stay in that *remote* or *barren* place any longer in Jesus name AMEN!

Chapter 6

Saying Goodbye to Death

When Jesus said to the Samaritan Woman in John 4:18, *for you have had five husbands, and you aren't even married to the man you're living with now.* The man that the Samaritan woman and I were living with now did not just wanted to be our husband he was also entangling us. And the man Jesus was talking about was death.

Why Death? The way The Holy Spirit revealed it to me this way. These *Five Husbands* were killing your spirit Madeline. *Rejection* had intimacy with you and then passed you to *Anger. Anger* then passed you to *Bitterness* and bitterness passed you to *Unforgiveness* and unforgiveness passed you to *Loneliness,* and finally loneliness passed you to *Death* and death was not only living with you but was laying a trap for you in your path.

Death, the action or fact of dying or being killed; the end of the life of a person or organism.

Psalm 18: 4-5 The ropes of death entangled me; floods of destruction swept over me. The grave wrapped its ropes around me; death laid a trap in my path.

THE ENTANGLE OF CONFUSION ARRIVES!

Entangled, to twist together or entwine into a confusing mass. I remember driving in my car after an argument with my family and my husband. I was crying so hard I felt like I was having a heart attack. My chest was so tight and I was saying inside my mind, I rather have a heart attack and die because I don't want to deal with this anymore. I am tired, I've lost it all and I don't have any strength to continue. I was so distraught that I remember calling my husband's grandmother and saying please take care of my daughters because I don't know what is going to happen to me. I remember her saying to me, "Madeline I love you, you are a special woman of God. Don't let Satan lie to you." While I was driving my car I was hoping someone would hit me. I walked in to the Hospital emergency room and told them I think I am having a heart attack and the nurse checked me and said, "You are fine."

I sat there and a voice deep inside me said, "What are you doing here? You are not going to die and you are not going to lose your mind because I am keeping you." See what I did not understand is that Jesus was keeping my mind even when I did not want to be kept. I was living and moving and existing because of Him!

Acts 17:28 For in Him we live and move and exist. As some of your own poets have said, We are his offspring.

~ 35 ~

THE VICTORY IS OURS!

1 Corinthian 15:57 How we thank God, who gives us the victory over sin and death through Jesus Christ our Lord.

Jesus had revealed himself to me and this Samaritan Woman as Hope of Glory. See that day in the Emergency Room, I felt hopeless but Jesus was showing me that there is hope and it is in Him. He is our Hope of Glory and there is going to be a positive outcome to the circumstances in my life.

Declaration!

I declare in the name of the Lord Jesus that if you feel right now that the spirit of Death has you entangled and Death is laying a trap for you, telling you there is nothing to live for or telling you, you are not going to make it because there is no Hope, I've come to tell you that is a lie. We have Victory over death through Jesus and you are not going to die you are going to live!

REPEAT WITH ME!

In Jesus name I loose myself from the ropes of death because Jesus died on the cross for me to have Victory over Death, and I will live and not die. I will live and not die, instead I will live to tell what the Lord has done for me.

Psalm 118:1 I will not die; instead, I will live to tell what the Lord has done.

~ <u>The Five Husbands That Don't Belong To You!</u> ~

Chapter **7**

Time to Take accountability

The Samaritan woman and I had to come to terms with ourselves and come to a point of accountability.

If I was ever going to receive freedom, healing and restoration it had to start with me taking accountability for myself first. When it comes to making a change, we never want Jesus to start with us first. I us to say, "Lord why can't you start with him, he did wrong." We always want to blame the other person. The word the Lord revealed to me was accountable.

Accountable means, *liable to being called to account, answerable required or expected to justify your actions or decisions.*

I remember the Lord revealed to me these words; He said, "Madeline my people are not free because they do not want to take *accountability* for decisions or actions." I had to answer Jesus the same way the Samaritan woman did in John 4:17, *I don't have a Husband, the woman replied.*

This Samaritan woman and I had to answer Jesus and say yes Jesus the *Husband of Rejection, Anger, Bitterness, Loneliness and Death* do not belong to me and I have no business being intimate with them. I had no business giving them my heart, my mind, my soul or my strength.

You say in your word Mark *12: 29-30 Jesus replied, The most important commandment is this Listen, o Israel! Listen you reading this book, The Lord our God is the one and only Lord. And you must love the Lord your God with all your heart, all your soul, all your mind, and all your strength.*

HE IS THE LORD OF MY LIFE!

The time had arrived to make God the Lord of my life again. To make someone your Lord means to make him your master and owner. What the Lord revealed to me was that these husbands were diluting the God in me! To *dilute* means, *to make weaker by adding another solvent*, and that solvent that *diluted* the God in me was *Rejection, Anger, Bitterness, Unforgiveness, Loneliness and Death.* I had made them Lord of my life and now it was time for these men to no longer be a part of my life. My life belonged to My Lord, God.

WEEPING MAY ENDURE FOR THE NIGHT
BUT JOY COMES IN THE MORNING!

I remember waking up that next morning after that hospital visit and just humbling myself on my bedroom floor and telling the Lord I don't want to do this with my strength anymore or my way. I need you to heal me. These *Husbands of Rejection, Anger, Bitterness, Unforgiveness, Loneliness and Death* have left me feeling ugly and I am tired of being harassed by these men. I was also tired of my daughters seeing me in that condition. I had allowed these men to kill me long enough. I remember screaming HEAL ME! HEAL ME! , HEAL ME!

2 Chronicles 7-14 AMP If My people, who are called by My name, shall humble themselves, pray, seek, crave, and require of necessity of My face and turn from their wicked ways, then will I hear from heaven, forgive their sin, and heal their land.

So I started to humble myself, pray, seek, crave and require the necessity of this Jesus to forgive my sin and heal my land.

TIME TO BREAK THE ILLEGAL COVENANTS AND DESTROY YOUR ENEMY!

Recently I was ministering at my local church and the Lord put this word in my heart, Illegal Covenants. It was so impactful to me because I have never heard these two words together or said them before. We thank God for His Holy Spirit that guides all truth.

The word *Covenant* means, agreement, *contract, pact, treaty.* The Holy Spirit said to me, "Madeline people make agreements, contracts and pacts with people and things that they have no business being in agreement or contract with."

The Samaritan woman and I got in agreement with Rejection, Anger, Bitterness, Unforgiveness, Loneliness and Death! And the Holy Spirit showed me that was an Illegal Covenant we had made with those Husbands.

Deuteronomy 5: 6-9 You shall have no other gods before me. You shall not make yourself a carved image any likeness of anything that is in heaven above, or that is in the earth beneath, or that is in the water under the earth; you shall not bow down to them nor serve them. For I, the Lord your God, am a jealous God.

GOD HAS ALREADY BROKEN THOSE ILLEGAL COVENANTS

Colossians 2-14 AMP Having cancelled and blotted out and wiped away the handwriting of the note (bond) with its legal decrees and demands which was in force and stood against us (hostile to us). This (note with its regulation, decrees and demands) He set aside and cleared completely out of our way by nailing it to (His) cross.

REPEAT with me!

Lord Jesus in Your name I break any illegal covenants I have made with *Rejection, Anger, Bitterness, Unforgiveness, Lonliness and Death.* Today, this is possible because Your word says that you took any illegal agreements that were against me and nailed them to the cross. So I am free from those Illegal Covenants and I make a covenant with You that I will have no other God before you!

Chapter 8

WHAT YOU DON'T DESTROY WILL
DESTROY YOU!

What the Lord revealed to me while writing this book is that these five Husbands needed to be driven out, not only from my life but my land and my surroundings. The Holy Spirit reminded me of *Numbers 33:55 But if you fail to drive out the people who lived in the land, those who remain will be like splinters in your eyes and thorns in your sides. They will harass you in the land where you live.*

~ 45 ~

IT WAS TIME TO DRIVE OUT THE MIDANITES!

What I realized is that in I order to receive true freedom, healing, restoration, I first had to drive out *Rejection, Anger, Bitterness, Unforgiveness, Loneliness and Death* from my land because they were still surrounding me! What is the land I am talking about? My territory, which is **My Mind, My Heart, My Soul** and everything I know the Lord has blessed me with, which is **My Home, My Marriage, My Children, My Finances and Belongings.**

STOP THE ENEMY FROM STEALING YOUR GRAIN!

The Holy Spirit took me to *Judges 6: 11, Then the angel of the Lord came and sat beneath the oak tree at Ophrah, which belonged to Joash of the clan of Abiezer. Gideon son of Joash had been threshing wheat at the bottom of a winepress to hide the grain from the Midianites.*

Gideon had no business being at the bottom of a winepress hiding from his enemy the Midianites. I looked up the meaning of the word Midianites. Midianites means *strife*, which means *angry or bitter disagreement over fundamental issues; conflict.* Gideon was at the bottom not only hiding from the enemy but hiding the grain (His Blessing) from his enemy the Midanites because they had brought him conflict before and stole everything from him.

The Lord told me, "Madeline it's time to stop hiding from the Midianites. I know they brought conflict to **your Mind, your Heart, your Soul and Home, Marriage, Children, and Finances,** but it's now time to destroy those Midianites. It's time to destroy *Rejection, Anger, Bitterness, Unforgiveness, Loneliness and Death.*"

Judges 6: 12, Then the angel of the Lord appeared to him and said Mighty hero, the Lord is with you.

Here is the Lord reminding me who I am in Him. I am a Mighty hero. He has called me to be the head and not the tail, to be above any situation and not beneath it and most important thing is He is with me! But for a second there I said exactly what Gideon said:

Judges 6: 13 Sir, Gideon replied, if the Lord is with us, why has all this happened to us?

I was saying Lord if You are with me why is all this happening to me? What the Lord revealed to me is that it was time to drive them out and completely destroy *Rejection, Anger, Bitterness, Unforgiveness,Lonliness and Death* once and for all. I left them in my land long enough. I had even gotten comfortable and familiar with them. What you get familiar with you may never destroy.

THANK YOU FOR THE VICTORY!

Judges 6-16 The Lord said to him, I will be with you. And you will destroy the Midianites as if you were fighting against one man.

You have to decide to pursue the Midanites so that they can no longer pursue you. So I CHALLENGE you, pursue *Rejection, Anger, Bitterness, Unforgiveness, Loneliness and Death* and kill them. You know why I say kill them? Because what is killed can never recover.

Judges 8:21, Then Zebah and Zalmunna said to Gideon Don't ask a boy to do a man's job! Do it yourself! So Gideon killed them both, see you have to decide to do this yourself and not be afraid because GOD is with you.

THE OUTCOME WILL BE PEACE!

Judges 8:28 That is the story of how the people of Israel defeated Midian, Which never recovered, throughout the rest of Gideon's lifetime.

How powerful is that, when you defeat your enemy to the point that they will never recover throughout the rest of your life! I call that victory! Like the Samaritan woman, I had to stop being a victim to *Rejection, Anger, Bitterness, Unforgiveness, Loneliness and Death* and decided to kill each and every one of them.

What does this bring? It brings freedom and to be *free* means *not under the control or in the power of another.* To see a manifestation of a positive outcome you can no longer be under the control of *Rejection, Anger, Bitterness, Unforgiveness, Loneliness or Death.*

Second it brings healing which means, to set right, repair. Jesus repairs any wound you received, whether the wounds were brought by someone's infidelity, adultery, physical abuse or verbal abuse, however the wound was caused. This healing is for you!

Third it brings you *restoration* which means *to return (someone or something) to a former condition, place, or position.* That means Jesus restores you back to him not only that He restores you but He restores **your Mind, your Heart and your Soul.**

Now that I've experienced the freedom, the healing and the restoration, I can say today I do not depend on the prescription drug the doctor gave me. I don't need it anymore. I don't depend on alcohol anymore to feel good. When I experienced the freedom, healing and restoration of Jesus, then and only then did Jesus set my marriage free from Infidelity. He then brought healing between me and my Husband and Restored My Marriage. All along I just needed this Man in my life, Jesus!

THE BELOVED REVEALED HIMSELF TO ME!

John 4: 25-26 The woman said, I know the Messiah will come- the one who is called the Christ. When he comes, he will explain everything to us. Then Jesus told her, I am the Messiah!

In Mathew 3:17, It says that a voice from heaven said, This is My Son, My Beloved, in whom I delight.

And I started to get to know Jesus as My Beloved, because *beloved* means *dearly loved or much loved person.* And I was falling in love with Jesus and started to love Him as a husband, as my Husband. Jesus arrived at the well where the Samaritan woman and I were and there He spoke to us tenderly and returned our joy again. He turned our valley of trouble into a gateway of hope and He freed us from the captivity of *Rejection, Anger, Bitterness, Unforgiveness, Loneliness, and Death.*

Hosea 2: 14-16 But then I will win her back once again. I will lead her into the desert and speak tenderly to her there. I will return her vineyards to her and transform the Valley of Trouble into a gateway of hope. She will give herself to me there, as she did long ago when she was young, when I freed her from her captivity in Egypt. When that day comes, says the Lord you will call me my Husband instead of my master.

IT'S TIME TO PRAISE HIM!

John 4:28 The woman left her water jar beside the well and went back to the village and told everyone, Come and meet a man who told me everything I ever did!

It was true what I had read all those times in *Isaiah 61: 1-3 that Jesus said The spirit of the Lord God is upon me, Because the Lord has anointed me to preach good tidings to the poor, He has sent Me tidings to the poor; He has sent me to heal the brokenhearted, To*

proclaim liberty to the captives, And the opening of the
prison to those who are bound; To proclaim the acceptable
year of the Lord, And the day of vengeance of our God; To
comfort all who mourn, To console those who mourn in
Zion, To give beauty for ashes, The oil of joy for
mourning, The garment of praise of praise for the spirit of
heaviness; That they may be called trees of righteousness.

Jesus made me a new woman.   He brought healing to my broken heart, He brought freedom to my captivity and He opened the door to my prison. He gave me beauty again He brought me comfort and consolation; He changed that spirit of *Rejection, Anger, Bitterness, Unforgiveness, Loneliness, Death* and gave me a spirit of praise. Why do I say Praise?   Because what was coming out of my mouth were words of gratefulness.

I am sure the people in the village were astonished with the Samaritan woman's change.   That is what started to happen to me, my husband and people around me would say I see a good change in you, you look different, you act different.   You are not the same Madeline. I remember every other time before when my husband would see me, I was angry and bitter, frustrated, wanting to argue, yelling and screaming. Now I was saying to him and everybody else come and meet a man who told me everything I ever did!

During that 2 year separation period, shame kept me from giving God any praise, but I no longer felt ashamed to face the world. Jesus was bringing me not just honor but double honor. Instead of feeling confused, I was rejoicing again and I possessed land as God opened the way for me to come back to my home. I was enjoying being a mother again. I was enjoying cooking and cleaning my home and I was actually experiencing peace in all areas of life. I remember I used to say I just want peace, I just want peace and I finally got it.

Romans 5:1 Therefore, since we have been made right in God's sight by faith, we have peace with God because of what Jesus Christ our Lord has done for us.

Did you see that? We have peace with God. say it aloud, I have peace with God. That means there is no true peace without him.

Chapter 9

GIVEN THE KEYS TO THE KINGDOM!

John 4:30 So the people came streaming from the village to see him.

S he had been a part of the *Five Husbands* that did not belong to her. But NOW she became a part of the Five Fold Ministry. I told you earlier the number five means undeserved acceptance. Jesus has accepted her as part of His church.

~ 57 ~

Ephesians 4:11 He is the one who gave these gifts to the church: the apostles, the prophets, the evangelist, and the pastors and teachers.

Do you see what happened here? She went from being rejected to accepted, from being full of anger to full of joy, from being bitter to good, from being full of unforgiveness to forgiving, from being lonely to satisfied, from being dead to being alive. I was done blaming my husband or the betrayal or other people, or the world for what had happened.

What enemy meant for evil, God turned it around for good; I was now able to say like Joseph in *Genesis 45-8 Yes, it was God who sent me here, not you!*

NO LONGER DEFECTIVE BUT EFFECTIVE!

Psalm 118:17 I will not die, but I will live to tell what the Lord has done.

This is how the Holy Spirit revealed it to me. *Defective* means, *an imperfection that causes inadequacy or failure; a shortcoming.* The definition of *effective* when used as a noun is, *a soldier fit and available for service.*

When Jesus arrived at that well, He was there to recruit me and this Samaritan woman to be effective in the Kingdom of God. The definition of *recruit* means, *enlist (someone) in the armed forces.* But you see it does not stop there when He recruited us because now this Samaritan woman and I became Recruiters for the Kingdom of God. She used that Five Fold ministry gift to equip other people. It became this Samaritan woman's responsibility and also my responsibility to have you to believe in Jesus.

One day in prayer the Lord was ministering to me saying, "Madeline I need people to be about My Father's business. God's business." I can imagine this Samaritan woman screaming out loud, I am not dead but alive to tell you what the lord has done!

John 4:39 Many Samaritans from the village believed in Jesus because the woman had said, He told me everything I ever did.

That is why the name of the ministry the Lord has given me is called Keys to the Kingdom. The definition of the word *key* is a *small piece of shaped metal, with incisions cut to fit the wards of a particular lock that is inserted into a lock and turned to open.*

In *Mathew 16:19* Jesus had told Peter one of his disciples, and *I will give you the keys of the Kingdom of Heaven. Whatever you lock on earth will be locked in heaven, and whatever you open on earth will be opened in heaven.*

I am using the those same keys that Peter was handed by Jesus to announce to you this; in the name of Jesus I unlock you from any *Rejection, Anger, Bitterness, Unforgiveness, Loneliness, Death.* It's the same key the Samaritan woman used in her village. I am using it now with you, be free in Jesus name!

BECOMING YOUR ENEMY WORST NIGHTMARE!

John 4:39-40 Many Samaritans from the village believed in Jesus because the woman had said, He told me everything I ever did! When they came out to see him, they begged him to stay for two days, long enough for many of them to hear his message and believe. Then they said to the woman, Now we believe because we have heard him ourselves, not just because of what you told us. He is indeed the Savior of the world.

How did the Samaritan woman become the enemy's worst nightmare? By standing up with a testimony in her mouth. It's the same thing I am doing today with this book you are reading.   I am sharing with you my testimony by telling you how He revealed to me how to pursue and kill *Rejection, Anger, Bitterness, Unforgiveness, Loneliness and Death* so they could no longer pursue and kill me.   He also set me free, healed me, and restored me. What a powerful testimony to declare, that you too can overcome. Because of this the Samaritan woman and I can show others how to overcome in Jesus.

Revelation 12:11 And they Overcame him by the blood of the Lamb and by the word of their testimony.

Chapter 10

TODAY IT STARTS WITH YOU!

John 4:28 The woman left her water jar beside the well and went back to the village and told everyone, Come and meet a man who told me everything I ever did!

TIME TO DROP THE WATER JAR!

Everyone says that they want to be happy. I know because I used to say the same thing. After all that I have been through I am telling you, you can be happy because your advocate Jesus has arrived! The definition of *advocate* is, *one* *who pleads on your behalf.* And Jesus is pleading right now on your behalf because He wants to set you free. Look at this story below.

Luke 13: 10-13 Now he was teaching in one of the synagogues on the Sabbath. And behold, there was a woman who had a spirit if infirmity eighteen years, and was bent over and could in no way raise herself up. But when Jesus saw her, He called her to Him and said to her, Woman, you are loosed from your infirmity. And he laid his hands on her, and immediately she was made straight, and glorified God.

What I've learned is that in order to see a manifestation of a positive outcome in your circumstance or your life, It starts with you first! Like I said before I never wanted to hear that. I wanted Jesus to start with everyone else but these Husbands that did not belong to me. These Husbands impact on my life had me bent over to the point that even if I tried I could not raise myself up.

I wanted to see the manifestation of a positive outcome in my life just like I know you do. But you have to let Him start with you! It says in this story that this woman had this condition for 18 years and this sickness had her bent over to the point that she could not raise herself up. This is how a lot of people live their daily lives, bent over unable to raise themselves up. I tell you that you no longer have to stay that way. Jesus has seen you and is telling "WOMAN BE LOOSED " let Him lay His hands right now on you so your life can be made straight and after He makes you straight, you will be able to give Glory to God. I challenge you today to let the Advocate set you free. Let Him start with you because those *Husbands named Rejection, Anger, Bitterness, Unforgiveness and Death* do not belong to You!

My Prayer for you!

Lord Jesus I pray that this book, this Testimony and this Revelation that you have had me write and share in this season be exactly what this person reading this book needs. I pray that every person that reads this book COMES OUT of any situation or circumstance that they may be facing TO SEE You Jesus, but not only see You but do the same thing the people in the village did. They BEGGED You Jesus to stay with them. They are able to say NOW I BELIEVE because we have heard for ourselves. It is not just because of what I read in this book, but it is because now I can say that Jesus is the Savior of the World. I pray that you will experience the Jesus of Salvation, Truth and Glory!

Announcing The First Kingdom Key Collection product. The Keys to the Kingdom glass reminds the world that God is still a God of Truth, Salvation ,Glory! Our product is available at <u>www.kingdomkey.com</u> and you can contact us by email at <u>kingdomkeycollection@me.com</u>

~<u>The Five Husbands That Don't Belong To You!</u> ~